CHILDREN'S DAY
PROGRAM BUILDER No. 9

Recitations—Exercises
Songs—Skits

Compiled by Evelyn Stenbock

Lillenas Publishing Co.
KANSAS CITY, MO. 64141

Welcome

We welcome you
   This Children's Day
To hear our songs
   And help us pray.
(*Bow heads and fold hands.*)
Thank You, God, for this
   Happy Children's Day.
          Amen.

—*Elizabeth Seatter Christensen*

Big Enough

I'm too small to cross the street
   All by myself
But I am big enough to find
   The cookies on the shelf.

I'm too small to comb my hair and
   Too small to go to school
But I am big enough to love Jesus
   And practice the golden rule.

—*Ruth Vaughn*

Not Too Small

I'm not too small,
   I'm glad to say,
To speak for Jesus
   On this day.

I can tell you that
   His love and care
Are for all people
   Everywhere.

—*Merle Glasgow*

Every Day

Jesus loves
   The children dear,
Every day
   Throughout the year.

—*Merle Glasgow*

Welcome

Welcome, everybody!
   We're very glad you came;
We all love Jesus
   And gather in His name.

—*Ruth Vaughn*

Happy Children's Day!

(*An exercise for six children*)

1ST CHILD—We can do a lot of things

2ND CHILD—Even if we're small.

3RD CHILD—Children's Day is here
          again

4TH CHILD—Bringing joy to all.

5TH CHILD—Now'll we'll open with a
          song,

6TH CHILD—Then to all we'll say—

ALL—Every one of you that's here,
   Happy Children's Day!

—*Christine E. Scott*

Much Good

I'm so young and tiny
  But here are my pennies, too.
I'm happy when I think
  Of the good they will do.

—Helen Kitchell Evans

Share Your Light

(Child carries lighted candle. On last line point to right, center, and left audience.)

Little candle,
  Share your light
With all the people
  Here tonight.

Help to spread
  The message true,
That Jesus loves all—
  You *(point)* and you *(point)* and
    you *(point)*.

—Merle Glasgow

Always

Jesus will love me always,
  Not just this Children's Day,
Because I'll always love Him
  And let Him lead the way.

—Helen Kitchell Evans

Hello!

(Child may raise hand to audience while speaking first line.)

Hello, dear people!

I hope I don't forget
  What I'm supposed to say,
I know it's real important
  On this special day.

One word I'm sure is "Welcome";
  Next is, "Glad you came!"
We hope each thing we say and do
  Will honor Jesus' name.

—Merle Glasgow

Best Book

(Child carries a Bible.)

This book is the Bible,
  Best Book of all.
I can't read the words,
  'Cause I'm too small.

But I know the words tell
  About Jesus, you see,
And God's loving care
  For you and for me.

—Merle Glasgow

A Sunbeam

A sunbeam I will be for Him,
  Spreading joy and cheer,
Because I am so happy
  Knowing God is near.

—Jean A. Zellers

My Small Way

I'm very small
  This special day,
So I'll speak to you
  In my small way.

I'm happy because
  I know it's true
That Jesus loves me,
  And He loves you!

—Merle Glasgow

Because

(For three small children.)

1st CHILD—This is our day to sing our
  songs,

2nd CHILD—And bring glad news your
  way,

3rd CHILD—And say our Bible verses,

ALL—Because it's Children's Day!

—Christine E. Scott

3

A Place for Me

I'm glad there's a place
For the size of me
To be a helper
In God's family!

—*Merle Glasgow*

God Is with Me

God is with me
Through the day,
In my work
And in my play.

God is with me
Through the night,
He keeps me safe
'Til morning light.

God is with me
Everywhere—
I thank Him for
His loving care!

—*Merle Glasgow*

Please Help Me, God

Please help me, God,
This happy day,
To use my hands
To help someway.

Please help me use
My eyes to see
Someone whose helper
I can be.

Please help me use
My feet to do
An errand needed
For someone, too.

Please help me use
My heart to share
Your love each day,
And everywhere.

—*Merle Glasgow*

I Love Him

(Child carries basket of flowers. Holds it up to audience.)

See what I brought
To God's house today?
It will make it beautiful
In a special way.

Jesus loved the flowers,
He talked about them, too.
That is why I brought them—
I love Him, don't you?

(Leave basket of flowers in any convenient place.)

—*Merle Glasgow*

Six Little Sunbeams

(For six small children. May be recited or sung to tune of "Ten Little Indians.")

One little,
Two little,
    Three little sunbeams,
Scatter
Love and
    Joy and cheer.
Four little,
Five little,
    Six little sunbeams,
Children's Day is here!

One little,
Two little,
    Three little sunbeams,
Smile and sing
    This happy day.
Four little,
Five little,
    Six little sunbeams,
Sharing love
    This way!

—*Merle Glasgow*

4

We Are Needed

(For a group of children)

1st Child *(boy)*—
I'm a leader;

2nd Child *(girl)*—
I'm a helper;

Both Children—
    We are needed for the work.

1st Child *(boy)*—
I'm a leader;

2nd Child *(girl)*—
I'm a helper,

Both Children—
    And our motto is, "Don't Shirk."

1st Child *(boy)*—
We need leaders;

2nd Child *(girl)*—
We need helpers,

Both Children—
    Who cooperate real well.

1st Child *(boy)*—
We need leaders;

2nd Child *(girl)*—
We need helpers;

Both Children—
    We've a story we must tell.

Group of Children—
Jesus calls to leaders, helpers;
    Spread the gospel, loud and clear.
Go forth to every nation
    Every day of every year.

—*Helen Kitchell Evans*

God's Flower

I'm a flower in God's garden;
    May I ever for Him bloom.
Showing life and beauty 'round me,
    Driving far away the gloom.

As the fragrance of God's roses
    Spread around their sweet perfume,
May I share the love of Jesus
    With each person in this room!

—*Jean A. Zellers*

A Good Feeling

It's a good feeling
    To know, you see,
That God always loves
    And cares about me.

He cares if I'm happy,
    He cares if I'm sad.
He cares when I'm good
    Or when I am bad.

Yes, it's a good feeling
    Wherever I go,
To know that God cares
    And loves me so!

—*Merle Glasgow*

5

Our Bible

(For a child who carries a Bible)

It seems that when I hold
The Bible in my hands
I feel God very near;
    It tells about His plans.

It tells us that He loves us
    Whether it's day or night.
I'm glad we have our Bible
    To teach us what is right.

—*Merle Glasgow*

I Look like Me!

My eyes are gray.
Tim's eyes are blue.
    Then oh! What a surprise.
For when we look
At our friend Kay,
    We see she has brown eyes.

My hair is brown.
Tim's hair is blonde.
    Kay's hair is black, you see.
Tim looks like Tim.
Kay looks like Kay.
    And I look just like me.

—*Aida Huber Shaw*

Love

(Child carries a card, kept hidden until the last line, with the word "love.")

If you give it away
    You have it each day—
Isn't it strange
    How it works that way?

Perhaps you've guessed
    Just what it might be—
It really works!
    I've tried it, you see!

(Holds up card) L-O-V-E, Love!

—*Merle Glasgow*

God Planned It All

For flowers to bloom
    And smell so sweet,
For grass to grow
    About our feet,
God planned it all.

For the sun to shine
    And the wind to blow,
For raindrops to fall,
    Then the bright rainbow,
God planned it all.

For trees to grow
    And give us shade,
For pools of water
    Where we can wade,
God planned it all.

For all these things
    God with us shares.
Let's say to Him
    Our "Thank You" prayers,
Because He planned them all.

—*Merle Glasgow*

Be Cheerful

Be a cheerful giver, friend;
    Rally to the call.
It takes a lot of money
    To carry the gospel to all.

—*Helen Kitchell Evans*

God's Flowers

(For a girl carrying flowers)

My garden blooms so brightly
    With flowers sweet and fair;
They love to show their beauty
    To people everywhere.

We are God's own flowers
    Planted by His love.
Let us show forth the beauty
    Of Christ who lives above.

—*Norma F. Gluhareff*

I Like God's Plan

I like God's plan,
So good and wise
    For me to work and play;
I like it too
Because I'm learning
    How to do things His way.

—Merle Glasgow

Thank You, God

(For four children)

1st Child—
For morning light
    Of each new day,
For time to work
    And time to play,

Unison—
Thank You, God.

2nd Child—
For friends and home,
    For parents, too,
For time to learn
    Things that are new,

Unison—
Thank You, God.

3rd Child—
For time to speak
    Kind words each day,
For time to learn
    More of Your way,

Unison—
Thank You, God.

4th Child—
For all Your plans,
    For loving care
And for Your love
    That we can share,

Unison—
Thank You, God.

—Merle Glasgow

I'm Glad

I'm so glad I can talk
    To God in my own way;
I can ask Him to help me
    Or, "Thank You," to Him say.

Sometimes I don't need
    To say words at all,
I just think about Him
    And His love for all.

—Merle Glasgow

Kind Deeds

Doing kind deeds
Is like planting seeds,
    In a garden of love each day.
First thing you know
They take root and grow—
    God just planned it that way!

—Merle Glasgow

Showing Love

1st Child—
We're showing love
When we are kind
    And speak words that are true.
We're showing love
When we can help
    With work that we can do.

2nd Child—
We're showing love
When we obey
    Our father and our mother.
We're showing love
When we help care
    For a baby brother.

3rd Child—
We're showing love
When a thank-you prayer
    To God each day we say,
For loving care
And for helping us
    To learn more of His way.

—Merle Glasgow

Being Me

Being me
  Is so much fun,
I won't trade places
  With anyone!

Being me
  Each bright new day
Is the way God planned—
  I like it that way!

       —*Merle Glasgow*

Today as Long Ago

I'm so glad that Jesus
  In the very long ago
Gathered children 'round Him
  Because He loved them so.

I'm glad we know today
  He loves children just as dear;
Though we can't see His face
  We know that He is near.

       —*Merle Glasgow*

Thank You

(For six children)

1st Child—
A penny isn't much,

2nd Child—
  A nickel not much more;

3rd Child—
A dime is still a little mite,

4th Child—
  But just start keeping score.

5th Child—
When all the coins are counted

6th Child—
  We find there's quite a few

Unison—
To send to all our missions,
  So to all we say, "Thank you."

       —*Helen Kitchell Evans*

Glad for Jesus

I'm glad for Jesus,
  How about you?
I love Him so much—
  He loves me, too.

He loves you, too *(point to audience)*,
  And wants you to be
A helper in
  His big family.

       —*Merle Glasgow*

Surprise for Miss Wilson

(A play for primary children.)

By Christine E. Scott

SETTING—
Children's Sunday school classroom. Small table at center with Bible, books, pictures, and large cards with colored pictures on front of Bible personalities, families, children, flowers, trees, etc. Chair for teacher at back of table. The time is the Sunday school hour, just before the Children's Day program.
(Enter four children, go to back of table, look at books, etc.)

1st CHILD—It's almost time for the Children's Day program. Miss Wilson will soon be here. Do you have your Bible verse ready?

2nd CHILD—I have mine! And here is the picture card that goes with it. *(Picks up card from table. Others find theirs.)*

3rd CHILD—When Miss Wilson asked us to find Bible verses on love for the program, I didn't know there were so *many!* *(Spreads arms indicating long list.)*

4th CHILD—Love is a very small word, but the meaning is big!

1st CHILD—And there are all kinds of love.

3rd CHILD—Like the love for our fathers and mothers.

2nd CHILD—And our church and Sunday school

4th CHILD—Our brothers and sisters.

3rd CHILD—And Miss Wilson, our teacher!

1st CHILD—In last week's lesson we learned how God shows His love to us, too.

2nd CHILD—In *thousands* of ways! Tiny leaves coming out in the spring—

4th CHILD—And flowers. And soft green grass!

3rd CHILD—Blue sky. And pink sunsets!

1st CHILD—The white snow in winter—each flake is different. A miracle!

2nd CHILD—And food to eat.

3rd CHILD—If we wrote everything down we'd need a pretty big sheet of paper!

4th CHILD—And a lot of pencils, too. *(Voices heard offstage.)*

1st CHILD—Here come the other children *(any number).*
(Children enter, each carrying large picture card.)

9

3RD CHILD—And Miss Wilson is coming to hear our verses on love.
(*Enter Miss Wilson, the Sunday school teacher.*)

MISS WILSON (*with happy smile*)—Good morning, everyone!

ALL—Good morning, Miss Wilson!

4TH CHILD—We're ready with our part for the Children's Day program, Miss Wilson.

MISS WILSON—There's time for one practice before we go into the church. Do you all have your cards?
(*The children stand in a row in front of the table. Each in turn holds up card with picture toward congregation and gives verse, speaking slowly and distinctly. Verses suggested are: 1 John 3:11; 1 John 3:18; 1 John 4:7; 1 John 4:11; Luke 6:27; Luke 10:27; John 3:16; John 13:34a; 1 Corinthians 13:1; 1 Corinthians 13:5; John 13:35; John 14:15; 1 John 4:21; 1 John 4:16a; 1 Corinthians 13:13.*)

MISS WILSON (*after last child speaks*)—But children! I thought you were going to *learn* your verses! But you were just *reading* them! From the backs of your picture cards! (*There is a pause, children smile and look at one another.*)

CHILDREN (*all together*)—Surprise, Miss Wilson! (*They all turn their cards showing they are blank on the back.*)

ALL—We weren't reading anything!

Our Sunday School's an Army

Our Sunday school's an army—
    Aren't you glad that you belong?
You must help to keep God's army
    Great, victorious, and strong.

Do your very best to conquer
    Sin wherever it may be,
Whether in your heart, your city,
    Or in lands across the sea.

Yes, our Sunday school's an army,
    Bravely fighting for the right;
And with Christ, the Lord, our Captain,
    We can always win the fight.

—*Dorothy Conant Stroud*

A Basket of Blessings

(For 10 children. First carries a basket filled with letters to spell the word "Blessings." The rest carry Bibles. Each child takes a letter before speaking and holds it up while speaking. Verses may be memorized or read.)

1ST CHILD—

Our basket is filled with blessings,
    They are written in the Bible, it's true.
God sends them down for everyone
And that includes me and you.

Now, we will share them with you,
    The ones we have chosen today.
We hope they will hold much joy
    For each of you, along the way.

B—

"By this shall all men know that ye are my disciples, if ye have love one to another" (John 13:35).

L—

"Let not your heart be troubled: ye believe in God, believe also in me" (John 14:1).

E—

"Every good gift and every perfect gift is from above . . ." (James 1:17).

S—

"Study to shew thyself approved unto God . . ." (2 Timothy 2:15).

S—

"Suffer the little children to come unto me, and forbid them not . . ." (Luke 18:16).

I—

"In all thy ways acknowledge him, and he shall direct thy paths" (Proverbs 3:6).

N—

"Now faith is the substance of things hoped for, the evidence of things not seen" (Hebrews 11:1).

G—

"God is our refuge and strength, a very present help in trouble" (Psalm 46:1).

S—

"Surely goodness and mercy shall follow me all the days of my life: and I will dwell in the house of the Lord for ever" (Psalm 23:6).

UNISON *(Spell it out together)*—
    B-L-E-S-S-I-N-G-S! Blessings!

(If desired, children may sing following verse to tune of "Jesus Loves Me.")
    B-L-E-S-S-I-N-G,
        In God's Word for you and me,
    We will find them there, you see,
        B-L-E-S-S-I-N-G!

—*Merle Glasgow*

His Glorious Creation

Choral Reading from Psalm Nineteen

READING DIVISIONS—
  Row One—One Reader
  Row Two—Two Readers
  Row Three—Three Readers
  Row Four—Four Readers
  Row Five—Five Readers
  (*The Readers may be placed according to size.*)

Row FIVE—The heavens declare the glory of God;

Row Two—and the firmament sheweth his handiwork.

Row ONE—Day unto day uttereth speech,

Row FOUR—and night unto night sheweth knowledge.

Row FIVE—There is no speech nor language, where their voice is not heard.

Row THREE—Their line is gone out through all the earth, and their words to the end of the world.

Row Two—In them hath he set a tabernacle for the sun,
  Which is as a bridegroom coming out of his chamber,

Row ONE—and rejoiceth as a strong man to run a race.

Row FIVE—His going forth is from the end of the heaven,

Row FOUR—and his circuit unto the ends of it:

Row ONE—and there is nothing hid from the heat thereof.

Row THREE—The law of the Lord is perfect, converting the soul: the testimony of the Lord is sure, making wise the simple.

Row ONE—The statutes of the Lord are right, rejoicing the heart:

Row Two—The commandment of the Lord is pure, enlightening the eyes.

Row THREE—The fear of the Lord is clean, enduring for ever:

Row FIVE—the judgments of the Lord are true and righteous altogether.

Row Two—More to be desired are they than gold, yea, than much fine gold:

Row THREE—sweeter also than honey and the honeycomb.

Row Two—Moreover by them is thy servant warned: and in keeping of them there is great reward.

Row One—Who can understand his errors? cleanse thou me from secret faults.

Row Three—Keep back thy servant also from presumptuous sins;

Row Two—let them not have dominion over me:

Row One—then shall I be upright, and I shall be innocent from the great transgression.

Rows Two and Five—Let the words of my mouth,

Row Four—and the meditation of my heart,

Row Three—be acceptable in thy sight,

Unison—O Lord, my strength, and my redeemer.

—Arranged by Carolyn R. Scheidies

Living for Christ

Choral Reading from Galatians Five and Six

Reading Divisions Beginning at Front—
 Row One—One Reader
 Row Two—Two Readers
 Row Three—Three Readers
 Row Four—Four Readers
 Row Five—Five Readers

Row One—Let him that is taught in the word communicate unto him that teacheth in all good things.

Row Two—Be not deceived; God is not mocked: for whatsoever a man soweth, that shall he also reap.

Row Three—For he that soweth to his flesh shall of the flesh reap corruption; but he that soweth to the Spirit shall of the Spirit reap life everlasting.

Row Four—And let us not be weary in well doing: for in due season we shall reap, if we faint not.

Row Five—As we have therefore opportunity, let us do good unto all men, especially unto them who are of the household of faith.

Row One—This I say then, Walk in the Spirit, and ye shall not fulfil the lust of the flesh.

Row Three—For the flesh lusteth against the Spirit, and the Spirit against the flesh: and these are contrary the one to the other: so that ye cannot do the things that ye would.

Row Two—But if ye be led of the Spirit, ye are not under the law.

Row Five—Now the works of the flesh are manifest, which are these; (*Speak one at a time*) (1) adultery, (2) fornication, (3) uncleanness, (4) lasciviousness, (5) idolatry,

Row Four (*speak one at a time*)—(1) witchcraft, (2) hatred, (3) variance, (4) emulations,

Row Three (*speak one at a time*)—(1) wrath, (2) strife, (3) seditions,

Row Two (*speak one at a time*)—(1) heresies, (2) envyings,

Row One—murders,

Row Three (*speak one at a time*)—(1) drunkenness, (2) revellings, (3) and such like:

Row Four—of the which I tell you before, as I have also told you in time past, that they which do such things shall not inherit the kingdom of God.

Row One—But the fruit of the Spirit is

Row Two (*speak one at a time*)—(1) love, (2) joy,

Row Three (*speak one at a time*)—(1) peace, (2) longsuffering, (3) gentleness,

Row Four (*speak one at a time*)—(1) goodness, (2) faith, (3) meekness, (4) temperance: (*All together*) against such there is no law.

Row Five—And they that are Christ's have crucified the flesh with the affections and lusts.

Row One—If we live in the Spirit, let us also walk in the Spirit.

Unison—Amen.

—Arranged by Carolyn R. Scheidies

Prayer for Church

How wonderful it is to have
A place to worship You;
A place to fellowship with friends
And study Your Word, too.

It may be small—it may be tall
With steeples, oh, so high
That reach up through the clouds
And point up to the sky.

Whatever kind of church we have,
We know that You are there
To listen to our praises
And hear our humble prayer.
Amen.

—Norma F. Gluhareff

Read It! Trust It! Pray!

The Bible is God's Word; do you
Believe that it is really true?
Then prove you do by just obeying
This good advice that I'll be saying:
Read it! Trust It! Pray!

If we but trust the Lord, we'll find
New peace for body, soul, and mind.
Just prayerfully, with open heart,
Read God's dear Word; He'll do His part
By showing you His way.

—Dorothy Conant Stroud

Song of Creation

Choral reading from Genesis, Chapters One and Two

READING DIVISIONS—
  Narrator
  God
  Group One—all male
  Group Two—all female

NARRATOR—In the beginning God created the heaven and the earth.

GROUP ONE—And the earth was without form, and void; and darkness was upon the face of the deep. And the Spirit of God moved upon the face of the waters.
  And God said,

GOD—Let there be light:

GROUP ONE—and there was light.

GROUP TWO—And God saw the light, that it was good:

NARRATOR—and God divided the light from the darkness.

GROUP ONE—And God called the light Day, and the darkness he called Night.

GROUP TWO—And the evening and the morning were the first day.
  And God said,

GOD—Let there be a firmament in the midst of the waters, and let it divide the waters from the waters.

GROUP ONE—And God made the firmament, and divided the waters which were under the firmament from the waters which were above the firmament: and it was so.

GROUP TWO—And God called the firmament Heaven. And the evening and the morning were the second day.
  And God said,

GOD—Let the waters under the heaven be gathered together unto one place, and let the dry land appear:

GROUP ONE—and it was so.

GROUP TWO—And God called the dry land Earth; and the gathering together of the waters called he Seas: and God saw that it was good.
  And God said,

GOD—Let the earth bring forth grass, the herb yielding seed, and the fruit tree yielding fruit after his kind, whose seed is in itself, upon the earth:

GROUP ONE—and it was so.

GROUP TWO—And the earth brought forth grass, and herb yielding seed after his kind, and the tree yielding fruit, whose seed was in itself, after his kind:

NARRATOR—and God saw that it was good.
And the evening and the morning were the third day.
And God said,

GOD—Let there be lights in the firmament of the heaven to divide the day from the night; and let them be for signs, and for seasons, and for days, and years:
And let them be for lights in the firmament of the heaven to give light upon the earth:

GROUP ONE—and it was so.

NARRATOR—And God made two great lights; the greater light to rule the day, and the lesser light to rule the night: he made the stars also.
And God set them in the firmament of the heaven to give light upon the earth.
And to rule over the day and over the night, and to divide the light from the darkness:

GROUP ONE—and God saw that it was good.

GROUP TWO—And the evening and the morning were the fourth day.
And God said,

GOD—Let the waters bring forth abundantly the moving creature that hath life, and fowl that may fly above the earth in the open firmament of heaven.

GROUP ONE—And God created great whales, and every living creature that moveth, which the waters brought forth abundantly, after their kind, and every winged fowl after his kind: and God saw that it was good.

NARRATOR—And God blessed them saying,

GOD—Be fruitful, and multiply, and fill the waters in the seas, and let fowl multiply in the earth.

GROUP TWO—And the evening and the morning were the fifth day.
And God said,

GOD—Let the earth bring forth the living creature after his kind, cattle, and creeping thing, and beast of the earth after his kind:

GROUP ONE—and it was so.

GROUP TWO—And God made the beast of the earth after his kind, and the cattle after their kind, and every thing that creepeth upon the earth after his kind: and God saw that it was good.
And God said,

GOD—Let us make man in our image, after our likeness: and let them have dominion over the fish of the sea, and over the fowl of the air, and over the cattle, and over all the earth, and over every creeping thing that creepeth upon the earth.

GROUP ONE—So God created man in his own image, in the image of God created he him; male and female created he them.

NARRATOR—And God blessed them and God said unto them,

GOD—Be fruitful, and multiply, and replenish the earth, and subdue it: and have dominion over the fish of the sea, and over the fowl of the air, and over every living thing that moveth upon the earth.
And God said,

GOD—Behold, I have given you every herb bearing seed, which is upon the face of all the earth, and every tree, in the which is the fruit of a tree yielding seed; to you it shall be for meat.
And to every beast of the earth, and to every fowl of the air, and to every thing that creepeth upon the earth, wherein there is life, I have given every green herb for meat:

GROUP ONE—and it was so.

GROUP ONE AND TWO—And God saw every thing that he had made, and, behold, it was very good.

NARRATOR—And the evening and the morning were the sixth day.

GROUP ONE—And on the seventh day God ended his work which he had made; and he rested on the seventh day from all his work which he had made.

GROUP TWO—And God blessed the seventh day, and sanctified it: because that in it he had rested from all his work which God created and made.

UNISON—Praise the Lord.

—Arranged by Carolyn R. Scheidies

Lord's Prayer Presentation

By Jane K. Priewe

(A presentation planned to teach children the Lord's Prayer and instill in them the importance of praying. Effectively given by 6th graders in children's church, or to the adult congregation.)

CHARACTERS—
 12 boy or girl disciples in costume
 1 Jesus figure
 3 readers

PRESENTATION

READER 1—Jesus loved His Heavenly Father. Jesus needed His Heavenly Father. Jesus talked to His Heavenly Father. Jesus prayed to His Heavenly Father. Many times Jesus asked His Heavenly Father to help Him. Jesus thanked His Heavenly Father for answering His prayers.

(Jesus comes from behind screen, or enters platform, kneels in front of audience, folds hands and bows head. Disciples follow and stand some distance away watching Jesus.)

READER 2—When the disciples saw Jesus kneeling with His hands folded and His head bowed, they knew He was talking to God. They knew He was praying, asking His Father for help, and thanking God for answering His prayers. Anytime . . . anyplace . . . Jesus prayed no matter where He was. When He prayed, the disciples often talked among themselves.

DISCIPLES—What's He saying?
    What's He praying about?
    Is He asking a favor of God?
    Is He thanking God for something?

READER 3—One day when Jesus was praying, Peter said,

PETER—Why don't we ask Jesus to teach us to pray?

DISCIPLES—Yes!
    I'd like that!
    Sure!
    Sounds good to me!
    Let's do it!

READER 1—When Jesus arose from praying and joined the disciples, John said,

JOHN—Master, will You teach us to pray? We want to know how to pray, too.

READER 1—Jesus answered,

JESUS—I'm happy that you men want to talk to My Father. Of course I'll teach you to pray. First, fold your hands. Now, bow your heads, and repeat this prayer after me. *(Disciples do as told.)*

JESUS—Our Father which art in heaven,

DISCIPLES—Our Father which art in heaven,

JESUS—Hallowed be thy name. *(Disciples repeat His words.)*
    Thy kingdom come.
    Thy will be done in earth as it is in heaven.
    Give us this day our daily bread.
    And forgive us our sins as we forgive those who sin against us.
    And lead us not into temptation;
    But deliver us from evil.
    For thine is the kingdom, and the power, and the glory for ever. Amen.

°Adapted.

18

READER 2—When the disciples said, "Amen," they looked up smiling, then arose to stand around Jesus. Andrew said,

ANDREW—Thank You, Master. That's a beautiful prayer! It says everything we need to pray about. But will Your Father in heaven hear us?

JESUS—Of course He will, Andrew. Because you believe in Me, God is *your* Heavenly Father. Because you love Me, God promises to hear and answer your prayers.

READER 3—James asked—

JAMES—May we say the prayer again with You, Jesus, so that we won't forget how to say it?
(Jesus nods, and all kneel to pray in unison, not repeating line for line as they did the first time. The prayer said, all disciples and Jesus stand.)

READER 3—When they had finished praying, Peter asked,

PETER—Master, may we teach Your prayer to those children? *(Points to audience.)*

JESUS—That's a fine idea, Peter. I hoped you would want to do just that. God loves the little children and so do I.
(Jesus, John, Peter, and Andrew move to the side, while nine disciples form a semicircle in front of audience. They hold 2 x 3-foot posters showing a picture which represents each petition. The side of the poster turned toward the disciple holds an explanation of the petition pictured on the front. Disciples step forward when their petition is being done.)

READER 1—I'll say a small part of the Lord's Prayer. Will you repeat it after me? Our Father which art in heaven . . . *(Disciples lead audience in repeating each petition.)*

DISCIPLE *(Steps forward holding card and reading from back)*—When we pray, "Our Father," we say, "Dear God, thank You for loving me as Your child, so that I can call You my Heavenly Father. You are everywhere, but heaven is where I think of You living, getting things ready for me to come and live with You."

READER 2—Hallowed be thy name. *(Repeat.)*

DISCIPLE—When we pray "Hallowed be thy name," we say, "God, because Your name is holy, I am asking You to help me so I won't say or use Your name in a wrong way. Let me sing and pray to You and say, 'Thank You.' "

READER 3—Thy kingdom come. *(Repeat.)*

DISCIPLE—When we pray, "Thy kingdom come," we say, "God, You let Your Son, Jesus, die to save us from our sins. Help us to teach and tell everyone this Good News."

READER 1—Thy will be done in earth as it is in heaven. *(Repeat.)*

DISCIPLE—When we pray, "Thy will be done in earth as it is in heaven," we say, "God, the angels in heaven obey You, so I ask You to help me obey You here in this world."

READER 2—Give us this day our daily bread. *(Repeat.)*

DISCIPLE—When we pray, "Give us this day our daily bread," we say, "Loving God, every day please give me the things I need to keep me alive and healthy, and help me not to worry."

READER 3—Forgive us our sins as we forgive those who sin against us. *(Repeat.)*

DISCIPLE—When we pray, "Forgive us our sins as we forgive those who sin against us," we say, "God, You promise to forgive my sins when I forgive people who sin against me. Help me to say I'm sorry when I do something wrong to another person."

READER 1—And lead us not into temptation. *(Repeat.)*

DISCIPLE—When we pray, "Lead us not into temptation," we say, "God, I need Your help to keep me from listening to the devil when he talks to me and tries to get me to do wrong."

READER 2—But deliver us from evil. *(Repeat.)*

DISCIPLE—When we pray, "Deliver us from evil," we say, "Dear God, keep reminding me that You are always with me, guarding and protecting me."

READER 3—For thine is the kingdom and the power and the glory for ever. Amen. *(Repeat.)*

DISCIPLE—When we pray, "For thine is the kingdom and the power and the glory for ever," we say, "God, You are strong! Everything in the whole world belongs to You and will always be Yours until the end of the world. Amen means, 'That's right, God, because You said so.'"

READER 1—Before we close we are going to sing the Lord's Prayer. Please listen carefully, and you will hear the same words we just taught you. Your part will be to sing the line, "Hallowed be thy name."

(Disciples sing "The Lord's Prayer," found in the back of this book.)
(The second time through, the audience joins in on the lines, "Hallowed be thy name.")

READER 2—Will you bow your heads and fold your hands? *(Prayer)* Thank You, Jesus, for teaching us such a beautiful prayer as the Lord's Prayer. Thank You, dear Heavenly Father for loving us and giving us Jesus. Thank You for answering our prayers, because we do love Your Son, Jesus Christ, and want to live to please Him. Amen.

(Children exit.)

The Ten Lepers

(A skit for junior children)

By Samuel H. Cox

CHARACTERS—

READER *(a junior girl)*
10 LEPERS *(junior boys)*
NEIGHBORING CAMPER *(junior girl)*

PREPARATION—

Set up a "campfire" in the center of the stage, using pieces of firewood and red plastic over a bulb (which should have a switch or chain). Arrange low, backless benches covered with dark blankets to appear as logs, sufficient space for 10 children to sit. The 10 lepers will wear old or ragged bathrobes. They should be barefoot, with smudges of burned cork on their faces and hands. The girl camper should wear a plain, faded cotton dress, quite long, beltless.

Scene I

READER—Jesus was in a hurry to keep an appointment in a certain village, and He was just descending the path that led into its outskirts when 10 men suddenly rose up in the trail before Him. They immediately cried out loudly the familiar cry of the leper, "Unclean, unclean!" and added quickly, "But Master, we would be made clean! Please heal us of this disease and make us clean!" They had heard about Jesus, the great Healer, and that is why they called Him Master. They were not aware, however, that the healer was Jesus, the Son of God—the Messiah.

Of course Jesus pitied them, for He loves everyone. He answered them: "Go show yourselves unto the priests." Then the Bible says that they went, and even as they walked toward their destination, they were healed of their leprosy!

The road to the Temple, however, was long and tedious, and the 10 cleansed lepers, in spite of their happy hearts, became weary. Besides, they were hungry (it was close to evening). So, seeing cool, shaded area by the side of the road, and the remains of a deserted campfire, they sat down on some logs and started to eat their lunches and to discuss the day's happy events.

(The 10 lepers enter. Reader continues without interruption. They sit on the logs and one quietly kneels by the fire to start it, by turning on the switch.)

Soon, however, their moods changed and they started to complain among themselves and worry about the future. They seemed to completely forget their debt to the One who had healed them. Only one of the 10 seemed to have a truly thankful heart.

1ST LEPER—

I think I shall never forget the day
When I first beheld the terrible gray
Of the dreaded leprosy I had found
On my hand! I knew I was bound!

With the dead I was bound to live among graves;
Yea, doomed to sleep with the rats in caves!
I was doomed to dirt and rags like these!
(Rises and looks at self.)
I had leprosy! What a dreadful disease!
(Shudders and sinks down to the log.)

10TH LEPER *(opposite end of log)*—

The rags, my friend, we can very soon burn!
Right now, I believe that we should return *(rises)*—
We should offer thanks to this great Man—
Quickly now! Let us go while we can!

(After a moment he sits down slowly, realizing no one intends to go with him.)

2ND LEPER—

I was rich before the day that I found
That by this sickness I also was bound.
Then I lost all—house, family, and land—
Because I was marked with the terrible brand!

10TH LEPER—

But friend, that is all now left in the past!
You are healed now. Come! You are free at last!
Let us arise now and go back to Him *(rises)*
Before the light of the day grows dim!
(Sits down again when no one moves to follow, shaking head sadly.)

3RD LEPER—

A merchant was I in the land of Dan.
When I discovered my spots, I ran!
Yes, I ran away from everyone!
I ran until I could no longer run.
And now I'm through! No more running for me!
The merchant's life is all I can see!

10TH LEPER (*rising*)—

    If no one goes with me, I go alone.
    I'm sick of this ceaseless, hopeless drone!
    (*Again sits down slowly after fourth leper begins to speak.*)

4TH LEPER—

    Hold on! Wait! I will go back with thee!
    But wait till the morning sun we see.
    Let us rest; the Healer we surely will find.
    In the morning we'll greet Him with clearer mind.

5TH LEPER—

    I'd like to return to painting once more;
    I was famous—rich—in the years before
    The blight struck me, and I left everything.
    But I'll get it all back and live like a king!

10TH LEPER (*leaping to his feet in excitement*)—

    A king, you say? Why of course! It was Him!
    The "King of the Jews" our salvation to win!

6TH LEPER—

    My family I left about 10 years ago.
    Now they are dead, I've no place to go!

10TH LEPER—

    With no place to go—why not follow Him?
    With Him there's joy, for each life, to the brim!

7TH LEPER—

    My home's in Gaza, the vineyards I tended.
    If I follow the Healer, this is all ended.

8TH LEPER—

    A fisherman I, my home by the sea
    Is quietly standing and waiting for me.

9TH LEPER—

    I watched the flocks in the valleys of Gad;
    I've always loved sheep since I was a lad.
    Soon I shall return. I'll shepherd a herd
    In the vales so green, as free as a bird!

10TH LEPER—

    The Healer is also a tender of sheep—
    "Good Shepherd" of men, He safely doth keep.
    But we have all wandered and gone astray!
    Now I shall arise and return—right away!
    (*Gets up and leaves in the direction from which they had come.*)

READER—This one man returned shouting the praises of God all the way back, until he found Jesus. When he had found the Lord, he threw himself down at His feet, crying out his gratitude with many tears of thanksgiving and devotion. For he knew, at last, that this was truly the Son of God.

Then Jesus said, "Were there not ten cleansed? But where are the nine? There were not found that returned to give glory to God, save this stranger." And He said unto him, "Arise, go thy way: thy faith hath made thee whole."

Meanwhile, the nine cleansed lepers *(still relaxing about the fire)* have found, to their horror, that their leprous spots have returned. They shed bitter tears of remorse, wishing that they had returned with the Samaritan to find Jesus and offer Him their lives. They were sorry, too, when they realized that they, the Jews—supposedly the religious leaders of the land—had shamefully complained, while he, of the despised Samaritan sect, had been the only one to act like a truly religious person.

Suddenly, they were surprised by a girl, whose parents had a campfire nearby. She apologized briefly for having listened in on their conversation from the very start.

GIRL—

Small wonder it is that your spots have returned!
Perhaps by now your lesson you've learned.
You've cried and you've grumbled about the sad past,
Forgetting the Lord who has healed you at last.

The advice I give now, you are wise to heed:
Arise, and take the Samaritan's lead!
When the Healer you've found, confess all your sin.
I'm sure He will heal you and cleanse you within.

The Healer, you see, is the Savior of men.
My father tells me He's coming again
To rule over all (after He has been killed,
And has risen again) as Jehovah has willed.
(They all rise quickly and return.)

Attacked by a Shaggy Dog!

By Evelyn Stenbock

(A skit for puppet and ventriloquist, or two puppets.)

PUPPET—Hey, _(name)_, look at all those children out there!

VENTRILOQUIST—Sure is a good crowd of good-looking kids, isn't it?

PUPPET—Well, I wouldn't say that.

VENTRILOQUIST—What do you mean? That's a real good crowd. It's Children's Day!

PUPPET—Yeah, I know. It's a good crowd.

VENTRILOQUIST—Well explain yourself! What do you mean, then?

PUPPET—I mean they're not good looking.

VENTRILOQUIST—_(name)_! That's a terrible thing to say! You'd better apologize!

PUPPET—Do I have to?

VENTRILOQUIST—You sure do. We won't go on with this program until you've told those children you're sorry!

PUPPET *(Pause, look around)*—Well . . . *(looks at children)* Well . . . I'm sorry you're not good looking.

VENTRILOQUIST—_(name)_! I don't know what I'm going to do with you!

PUPPET *(Looks at children again)*—Sorry! *(Laughs.)*

VENTRILOQUIST—You were gone over the weekend, _(name)_. Where were you?

PUPPET—Visiting a good friend.

VENTRILOQUIST—Oh, that was nice.

PUPPET—No it wasn't.

VENTRILOQUIST—It wasn't?

PUPPET—Nope.

VENTRILOQUIST—You mean you didn't have a good time?

PUPPET—I had a rotten time!

VENTRILOQUIST—Rotten! Well, what happened? I thought you said this was a good friend.

PUPPET—Well, yes, but . . .

VENTRILOQUIST—Didn't you like staying in her home?

PUPPET—I was attacked by a big dog! *(Loudly)* Big, mean, ferocious, horrible, shaggy dog!

VENTRILOQUIST—Oh, my goodness! That was terrible! Did it bite you?

PUPPET—Did it bite me? *(Looks at partner in disgust.)*

VENTRILOQUIST—Well, tell me what happened.

PUPPET—I was sitting there in my easy chair, minding my own business . . .

VENTRILOQUIST—Just sitting there, eh?

PUPPET—Yeah. Well, this big, shaggy dog came in the door and I said, "Hey! old ugly Shaggy Dog!"

VENTRILOQUIST—Oh, no, _(name)_! You shouldn't speak to strange dogs!

PUPPET—I shouldn't? You told me to be friendly.

VENTRILOQUIST—I told you to be friendly with boys and girls. You have to watch out for dogs. You have to find out first if they're friendly.

PUPPET—This one wasn't.

VENTRILOQUIST—He wasn't?

PUPPET—Nope. He sure wasn't. He lumbered across the room and started sniffing me. My heart almost stopped beating. Man, was I scared!

VENTRILOQUIST—I should think so!

PUPPET—All of a sudden he started nipping me, and I began to scream: "Help! Help! Leave me alone! Get away! Help!"

VENTRILOQUIST—And then what?

PUPPET—He opened his huge mouth real wide *(open puppet's mouth wide)* And . . . *(pause for effect)*

VENTRILOQUIST—Go on!

PUPPET—And he *(lots of expression)* grabbed me by the stomach and started to shake me!

VENTRILOQUIST—Oh, no! Poor _(name)_.

PUPPET—I let out one ter-r-rible scre-e-am of anguish! *(Scream.)*

VENTRILOQUIST—_(name)_! Not so loud!

PUPPET—Just when I thought I was a real goner, my friend rescued me!

VENTRILOQUIST—You mean your friend heard your screams and came running?

PUPPET—You'd better believe it. She ran into the room and grabbed that shaggy dog by the hair!

VENTRILOQUIST—And he let go of your stomach.

PUPPET—No, he didn't. He just held on. Those big teeth clamped together like a vise and sank deeper into my stomach!

VENTRILOQUIST—Oh, no! What did she do? Call for help?

PUPPET—She kept shouting, "Barney! Drop that puppet! Barney, drop it! Barney! That is not a cat!" (Pause.) He thought I was a cat.

VENTRILOQUIST—You mean the dog doesn't like cats and he thought you were one.

PUPPET—I guess so. Then she put her (expressively) soft, tender, beautiful, fragrant, gentle hands (loudly) right between his big teeth and yelled, "Drop him this minute or I won't buy you any more doggy biscuits!"

VENTRILOQUIST—Poor __(name)__! Did he let go?

PUPPET—Finally, finally she pried his jaws open and pulled me free!

VENTRILOQUIST—Boy, that was a close call.

PUPPET—It sure was. He killed a cat once!

VENTRILOQUIST—Well, I guess you really thanked your friend for rescuing you.

PUPPET—I sure did! __(name)__, know what I thought about after it was all over?

VENTRILOQUIST—What did you think about?

PUPPET—A Bible verse.

VENTRILOQUIST—Really? What verse?

PUPPET—1 Peter 5:8. (Quoting it.) "Be sober, be vigilant; because your adversary the devil, like a roaring lion, walketh about, seeking whom he may devour."

VENTRILOQUIST—And what did that make you think about?

PUPPET—Jesus. I remembered that Jesus is always nearby, ready to rescue us from danger, and all we need to do is call on Him. Jesus is really a good Friend.

VENTRILOQUIST—He sure is.

PUPPET—I wonder if all those boys and girls know Jesus? Maybe you'd better ask them, __(name)__. They sure need Him.

VENTRILOQUIST—That's right, they do need to know Jesus as their best Friend.

PUPPET—Well, why don't you tell them how they can get saved?

VENTRILOQUIST—(Give simple explanation of the gospel and the type of invitation you think is suited to your audience. Or, have the puppet ask the pastor or children's church leader to do so.)

Be Ye Kind

Adapted from Eph. 4:32 by P.W. and D.W.

Paul and Donna Williams

Be ye kind one to an-oth-er, be ye kind.____

____ Be ye kind one to an-oth-er, be ye

kind. Be ten-der-heart-ed, for-giv-ing one an-oth-er Ev-en as

God for Christ's sake has for-giv-en you.

Fine

Be ye kind one to an-oth-er, be ye kind.

Optional interlude
* Rhythm instruments   *cresc. gradually to the end*

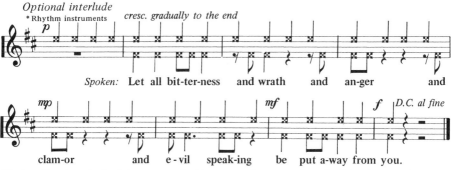

Spoken: Let all bit-ter-ness and wrath and an-ger and clam-or and e-vil speak-ing be put a-way from you.

*Begin with a drum in the 1st measure and add one more instrument in each of the six succeeding measures.

Ask, Seek, Knock

Adapted from Matthew 7:7-8 by D.S.   David Steele

Ask, seek, knock.(My Je-sus said) Ask, seek, knock. (My Je-sus said) Ask and it shall be giv-en to you; knock and it shall be o-pened to you.__ Seek, seek and ye shall find. Yes, ask, seek, knock. (My Je-sus said) knock. Ask, seek, knock.

The Lord's Prayer

Adapted from Matthew 6:9-13

West Indies tune
Arr. by Lyndell Leatherman

And for-give us, Fa-ther, all our debts; Hal-low-ed be Thy
A - men, a - men, it shall be so.

name. As— we for-give— all our debt-ors; Hal-low-ed
A - men, a - men, it shall be so.———

be Thy name. O Lord,— Hal-low-ed be Thy name.

God Needs Helpers

Kathryn Blackburn Peck

Faith Chambers Wilson

1. God needs help-ers, will-ing help-ers, Bus-y all the days,
2. God needs help-ers, man-y help-ers, There is much to do,

Help-ing moth-ers, help-ing oth-ers In all sorts of ways.
Mak-ing oth-er peo-ple hap-py. I will help. Will you?

What Shall We Children Bring?

Anonymous
From *The Book of Praise for Children,* 1881

Dennis Allen

1. The wise may bring their learn-ing, the rich may bring their wealth; And
2. We'll bring Him hearts that love Him; We'll bring Him thank-ful praise, And
3. We'll bring the lit - tle du - ties we have to do each day; We'll

some may bring their great-ness, and some bring strength and health. We, too, would
young souls meek-ly striv-ing to walk in ho - ly ways. And these shall
try our best to please Him at home, at school, at play. And bet - ter

bring our treas-ures to of - fer to the King; We have no wealth or
be the treas-ures we of - fer to the King; And these are gifts that
are these treas-ures to of - fer to the King Than rich - est gifts with-

1-2 D.C. 3

learn - ing: what shall we chil - dren bring?
e - ven the poor-est child may bring.
out them; yet these a child may bring.